What Is
Black Lives
Matter?

What Is
Black Lives
Matter?

by Lakita Wilson

illustrated by Gregory Copeland

Penguin Workshop

To Alonzo Pigatt Jr. May you live a long, joyful life, standing strong in your beautiful Black skin. Mommy loves you—LW

PENGUIN WORKSHOP
An imprint of Penguin Random House LLC, New York

First published in the United States of America by Penguin Workshop,
an imprint of Penguin Random House LLC, New York, 2021

Visit us online at penguinrandomhouse.com.

Library of Congress Cataloging-in-Publication Data is available.

Printed in the United States of America

ISBN 9780593385883 (paperback)   10 9 8 7 6 5 4 3 2 1 WOR
ISBN 9780593385906 (library binding)   10 9 8 7 6 5 4 3 2 1 WOR

Contents

What Is Black Lives Matter?

On February 26, 2012, seventeen-year-old Trayvon Martin left his father's girlfriend's home, in a gated community in Sanford, Florida, to get a quick snack. He purchased a bag of Skittles and an Arizona Iced Tea. Throwing his dark gray hoodie over his head to protect himself from the rain, Trayvon walked home.

As Trayvon made his way back into his quiet community, a man named George Zimmerman watched him from his car and reached for his cell phone. Over the last several years, George had called the police many times to report people in his neighborhood. However, every "suspicious" person George reported was a Black male.

"We've had some break-ins in my neighborhood," George told the police dispatcher. "And there's a real suspicious guy. This guy looks like he's up to no good or he's on drugs or something."

The dispatcher asked George questions as his car door creaked open. "Are you following him?" she asked. "We don't need you to do that."

George answered, "Okay."

But he left his car and continued following Trayvon on foot. Cornering him, George began to harass the teenager, and a fight began. Moments later, shots rang out, and seventeen-year-old Trayvon Martin fell to the concrete sidewalk, his bag of Skittles still tucked safely in his pocket, only seventy yards from his destination.

Trayvon Martin was a teenager who loved video games and fixing things. He liked trying new things like snowboarding and visiting New York City to see a Broadway play. He had dreams of becoming a pilot someday. Instead, Trayvon was gunned down before he even had the opportunity to attend his high-school prom. And the man who killed him was still free to walk around his gated community, patrolling for more "suspicious people."

Disappointment rippled through the Black community. In the United States, there is a history of treating Black lives like they don't matter. Many people who commit crimes against Black people are not punished for their actions. Fifty-seven years before Trayvon Martin's death, two white men in Mississippi killed fourteen-year-old Emmett Till after a white woman accused him of flirting with her. Emmett's killers were found not guilty. Twenty-one years before Trayvon's death, in Los Angeles, a Korean convenience-store owner shot fifteen-year-old Latasha Harlins to death after accusing her of stealing a bottle of orange juice. A California jury decided that Latasha's killer was guilty, but a judge only sentenced the shop owner to five years of probation.

The Black community demanded justice for Trayvon so strongly that his death made national news. The police finally arrested George Zimmerman, but he claimed self-defense, and in 2013, he was found not guilty of murdering Trayvon.

The evening after the George Zimmerman verdict, community organizer Alicia Garza posted a letter to Black people on Facebook. She wrote, "I continue to be surprised about how little Black lives matter." Alicia urged everyone in her community to stop giving up on Black life.

Then she ended her post by affirming,

"I love you. I love us. Our lives matter." Later, Alicia's friend, Patrisse Cullors, changed the last three words into the now famous hashtag: #BlackLivesMatter.

CHAPTER 1
Three Friends Start a Movement

Alicia Garza was born on January 4, 1981, in Los Angeles, California. She lived with her mother, stepfather, and younger brother, Joey. When Trayvon Martin was killed, Alicia, then thirty-one years old, thought about her younger brother. Trayvon had been racially profiled—or targeted because he was Black. Joey was tall and had brown skin and curly hair. Someone could racially profile him—just like they had Trayvon. Alicia felt powerless in that moment. But in reality, Alicia had been full of power since she was a child.

Alicia's mother began teaching her self-defense moves in their kitchen late at night when she was young. She told Alicia she didn't have to

Alicia Garza

do anything with anyone if she didn't want to. Alicia's mother had been attacked when she was younger, and she wanted her daughter to understand how to protect herself.

When Alicia was twelve, she thought a lot about protection. All around the country, adults argued about what teenagers should do with their bodies. Many adults felt like teenagers were too young to make their own health decisions. But Alicia believed teenagers had a right to protect themselves and their bodies. She fought to bring health education and resources to middle and high schools in her district—and she won. This was Alicia's first time organizing—and she found great power in seeing a problem and making a plan for change.

In college, Alicia joined the student association at University of California San Diego. There, she fought for higher pay for the university janitors. As an adult, Alicia worked as the special projects director for the National Domestic Workers Alliance. This organization fights to make sure labor workers like nannies, housekeepers, and caregivers are treated fairly on the job. Alicia's efforts supporting people who needed protection would help her later with her activist work.

Patrisse Cullors was born in Van Nuys, California. Living with her mom, sister, and two brothers in a low-income neighborhood had its challenges. Patrisse was nine when she saw her eleven- and thirteen-year-old brothers slammed into a wall by police officers. She was thirteen when she saw Los Angeles police handcuff and haul away her older brother Monte.

The problem was that Monte suffered from schizoaffective disorder, a mental health condition that affects the way a person thinks, feels, and behaves. Instead of helping Monte,

Patrisse Cullors

police officers often put him in jail. When Patrisse got older, Monte started writing her letters from   jail. He explained that he was beaten and forced to drink toilet water by county sheriffs who patrolled the jails. One time in 1999, he was almost killed. Patrisse and her mom wanted to tell someone—but there was no one to turn to. The police, in most cases, were always believed—especially over the word of a poor person with brown skin.

By the time she was twelve years old, Patrisse knew she was queer—a word used to describe someone who does not identify as straight or whose gender identity does not fully match the sex (male or female) they were assigned at birth. She was also part of the Jehovah's Witness religion. The elders in her faith community believed being queer was wrong. Patrisse knew she and her family would be shunned by the Jehovah's Witness community if she openly identified as queer. But at age sixteen, she came out to her family anyway and left home.

Young and on her own, Patrisse struggled to survive without much support. This showed her the importance of sticking up for everyone—even if they were poor, queer, or Black or Brown women.

When Patrisse was seventeen, she joined the Bus Riders Union, a group in Los Angeles that pushed for more funding for the bus system and less money for the city train system. Cutting bus funding meant poor people who lived in the city, those without cars and who didn't live near train stations, had fewer options to travel to places they needed to go, like grocery stores. In Patrisse's eyes, the people who were most often forgotten, like bus riders, were Black and poor.

In 2012, Patrisse started Dignity and Power

Now—a coalition that fights against brutality by sheriff's deputies who work inside the county jails. Patrisse's work supporting people who weren't often respected or treated fairly by those in power, including inmates, would help her as an activist later in life.

Opal Tometi was born on August 15, 1984, in Phoenix, Arizona. Opal's parents had been born in Nigeria. They came to the United States to build a new life as immigrants. Life in Phoenix, Arizona, for Opal and her two younger brothers was filled with community spirit. The Tometi family and other Nigerians in Phoenix formed a small community where they learned to stick together and look out for one another. Some of the Nigerians in Opal's community were immigrants like her parents. Others had been born in the United States like Opal and her brothers. Either way, everyone supported one another. Once, Opal's uncle

Opal Tometi

was sent to an immigration detention center. Members of the Nigerian community, whether they were family or not, took turns visiting Opal's uncle on weekends. This was their way of making sure the uncle was safe. It also let him know that he was loved and supported. This incident taught young Opal the importance of supporting one another to protect against unfair systems.

Opal had even heard of African immigrant men like Amadou Diallo and Mohamed Bah, who were killed by New York City police officers. It didn't seem to matter whether you had been born in this country or not. People with dark skin were being harmed and even killed. Opal believed that *every* Black person was worthy of respect. She also believed in safety in numbers and in unity. She felt Black immigrants and Black Americans working together to push back against racism could make a bigger difference. As an adult, Opal used her experiences as a Nigerian American to become an immigration activist.

Alicia and Patrisse met at an activist meeting as young adults. Later, they met Opal at a leadership training program for Black organizing. The three women kept in touch over social media. The night George Zimmerman was found not guilty of Trayvon Martin's murder, Alicia, Patrisse, and Opal decided to organize a new movement. But

the movement wouldn't be an overnight success. The Black Lives Matter movement began with three friends who wanted change. They started small—but placed big importance on working together.

CHAPTER 2
Another Black Life Lost

Two years after Trayvon Martin's murder, tragedy struck again. On August 9, 2014, eighteen-year-old Michael Brown and a friend walked down a two-lane street in their Ferguson, Missouri, neighborhood. A police officer pulled up in his squad car. The police officer told them to use the sidewalk.

Words were exchanged between Michael and the police officer. Neighbors heard yelling—and then they heard gunshots. Officer Darren Wilson had shot and killed Mike Brown.

When people questioned what happened, no one could believe it. Mike wasn't carrying a knife. He didn't have a gun. After the police officer shot Mike Brown, the teen put his hands up to surrender. And the officer shot him again.

Michael Brown

More than six hundred angry neighbors spilled from their nearby apartments. They immediately lashed out at police.

"Cover him up," neighbors yelled.

Michael's grandmother rushed to the scene. She asked the police officers what happened. But no one told her anything.

The crowd of neighbors grew angry. "My grandson never even got into a fight," Michael's grandmother said.

By early Saturday evening, neighbors began leaving candles, rose petals, and stuffed animals in the middle of the street. Michael Brown wasn't supposed to die like this. He had so many more years to live. Sadness filled the air.

On August 11, 2014, two men told reporters that they had seen Michael's hands raised high when the officer fired his gun multiple times.

Three weeks later, Patrisse Cullors and others organized the Black Life Matters Ride.

They gathered more than five hundred Black protesters from all over the country. Together, the group traveled by bus from many cities, including Chicago, Nashville, and Boston, to support the people of Ferguson. The protesters were journalists, lawyers, pastors, students, and other organizers. They all wanted one thing—justice for Mike Brown. The youngest rider was Nia Alvarez-Mapp. She was seventeen, only one year younger than Mike Brown. "Everyone thinks I'm crazy for doing this," Nia said, eating a Rice Krispies Treat, "but I don't want to [feel] fear when my back is turned."

After the protesters got off the bus, they gathered at the Ferguson police station. People of all colors were already there. Black, Brown, White, and Asian people held signs and shouted, "Hey, hey, ho, ho—racist cops have got to go!" and "Who am I? Mike Brown!"

Raising both hands high in the air, the

protesters shouted, "Hands up, don't shoot." They chanted this over and over to remind police officers that they weren't a threat—and Mike Brown hadn't been, either. Video footage of this

moment appeared on social media. People all over the country posted pictures of themselves with their hands raised over the hashtag #HandsUpDontShoot.

While the protesters chanted, a row of police officers stood silently with their arms crossed. They wore their uniforms and dark sunglasses. Uneasiness lingered in the air. The officers stared at the protesters, hoping they would tire themselves out.

The protesters were tired—of Black people dying in the streets. They refused to rest until they saw change.

The Ferguson protests weren't just about Mike Brown. The protesters wanted to let the world know that what had happened to Mike Brown was also happening to Black people all over the country.

Inspired by the protesting in Ferguson, Black Lives Matter cofounders Alicia Garza, Patrisse Cullors, and Opal Tometi returned home. They began planning ways to make their message reach across the country and all over the world.

CHAPTER 3
All Black Lives Matter

Before traveling to Ferguson, Alicia, Patrisse, and Opal were already making their voices heard. Opal set up the social media accounts. She encouraged Twitter users to share stories explaining why Black lives mattered. Alicia made protest signs and put them in the window of a local shoe shop. Patrisse marched down Rodeo Drive in Beverly Hills with a banner that read #BlackLivesMatter. She encouraged the customers shopping and having lunch to take a moment of silence to remember the Black lives lost to police brutality.

And after returning home from the Black Life Matters Ride, the three friends worked on growing their movement. Years ago, becoming an

activist meant you had to be a respected member
of your community and you were most likely
male. But Alicia, Patrisse, and Opal decided the
Black Lives Matter movement would be open
to all. They sent the message "Come as you are"

to their followers on social media. That meant
everyone was invited—no matter their gender,
sexual orientation, religion, age, race, style of
dress, or way of talking. They made sure to post
photos of activists dressed in everyday clothes

and in work uniforms to support the idea that anyone can and *should* be a part of the *people's* movement.

Next, Patrisse helped organize twenty-seven local Black Lives Matter chapters—twenty-six in the United States and one in Toronto, Canada. Alicia and Opal traveled to help support the new local chapters. By establishing local leaders to manage these chapters, the three founders were able to work on creating a strong mission statement for the Black Lives Matter movement.

The founders worried history would forget about Black women and queer and trans people when discussing the Black Lives Matter movement in the future. They were also concerned that the movement might only be associated with tragedy and sadness. So they created four key points that focused on Black justice *and* Black value. Their first and second key points included Black lives that had been previously ignored or mistreated in the Black community. This included women, queer and trans people, undocumented immigrants, and people with criminal records. The third key point planned to make sure that Black lives were no longer the targets of harm. The last key point focused on Black joy and Black contributions to society.

Online, Opal kept the #BlackLivesMatter hashtag going by asking people to share personal stories. However, as the hashtag went viral on social media, some people began pushing back against the organization. They claimed the Black Lives Matter movement excluded other groups. Other hashtags popped up. #BlueLivesMatter supported police officers. #AllLivesMatter felt activists should focus on supporting all races. However, people who used those hashtags rarely focused on Black justice. Instead, they focused on feeling left out. #BlackLivesMatter didn't mean that Black people didn't care about other races. Activists were simply calling attention to the fact that in the United States—and around the world—people had forgotten that Black lives mattered, too. The Black Lives Matter movement made it their mission to help the world remember.

CHAPTER 4
The Turning Point

On May 25, 2020, nine minutes and twenty-nine seconds changed the world forever. George Perry Floyd Jr. drove to a grocery store in Minneapolis, Minnesota. He made a purchase with a twenty-dollar bill. The store clerk believed the bill was fake and called the police.

Shortly after, police officers approached Floyd's vehicle. They asked him to get out of his truck. After putting George in handcuffs, the officers sat George on the sidewalk. They asked him if he was on drugs. George said no. The officers accused George of acting strangely. But witnesses claimed George looked calm, and they had even overheard him saying thank you. As officers walked George to their police car,

George Floyd

he fell to the ground. When they picked him up, he complained of not feeling well. He had just recovered from COVID-19, an illness that affects a patient's ability to breathe. George asked to lie on the ground, since small spaces like the back seat of cars scared him.

While George lay on his stomach, with his cheek pressed to the pavement, Officer Derek Chauvin kneeled down and pressed his knee into George's neck. Witnesses began pulling out their cell phones. They had seen these types of incidents on the news before. They knew that recording was important so no one could make up what *actually* happened that day.

At one point, three officers pressed down on George's body. One officer pressed his knee into George's neck. Another officer pressed down on his back, and one more held down his legs. As witnesses continued taping, an officer ordered them to leave.

Over and over, George cried, "I can't breathe," while citizens shouted, "You got him down. Let him breathe!"

"Please," George pleaded. "The knee in my neck, I can't breathe."

"Don't kill me," George begged. By this time, George was bleeding from his nose and mouth. Officers called for an ambulance, but they said it was a nonemergency. This made it take longer for the ambulance to arrive.

Meanwhile, George begged for water and told the officers that he was in pain everywhere on his body. When witnesses demanded the officers get George off the ground, one of the officers said George was "talking, he's fine."

Officer Derek Chauvin pulled out Mace to keep bystanders away as the other officers forced them from coming closer. Witnesses backed up but continued to plead with the officers to stop. One yelled out, "Check his pulse."

When an officer checked Floyd's wrist, he found no pulse. The officers still refused to help George. One officer did ask Officer Chauvin if they should move George onto his side, but Officer Chauvin responded, "No."

When the Hennepin County ambulance arrived, George was silent and not moving. Officer Chauvin's knee was still pressed on George's neck. The ambulance took George to the hospital, but he was pronounced dead when he arrived there.

The officers handling George's arrest filed their police report. They wrote that George had resisted arrest. They mentioned nothing about Officer Chauvin's knee on George's neck.

But hours later, cell phone videos began popping up on social media. Many witnesses shared their videos of what had happened to George so the world would know the truth. More and more people saw the footage, including the

Minneapolis Police Department. They asked the FBI to step in and investigate. The FBI made George's case a top priority. They found that the police officers had violated George's human rights. They promised criminal charges would be brought against the police officers responsible.

Meanwhile, as people watched what the officers did to George Floyd, they began gathering at the location where he had been killed. People left flowers, cards, and signs to honor George's life. Soon, the memorial spot became a place to protest. Hundreds of people marched to a nearby police station. Protesters carried signs that read "Justice for George," "I Can't Breathe," and "Black Lives Matter."

For two months, people everywhere had been staying home to help stop the spread of COVID-19, the coronavirus disease that had swept across several countries and affected people on almost every continent.

Violence against Black people was nothing new. But with the world at a standstill, large numbers of people had time to watch the unjust deaths of Breonna Taylor and Ahmaud Arbery—and now George Floyd—as the events unfolded on television news and social media. Breonna had been sleeping in her bed when she was murdered. Ahmaud was jogging in his neighborhood.

George was shopping at a grocery store.

Inspired by photos and video clips they saw on social media, many people decided to put on their masks, leave their homes during the pandemic, and protest in the streets of their hometowns. More peaceful protests cropped up in over two thousand cities in the United States and then in over sixty countries around the world.

Some city officials enforced curfews, making the protesters leave the streets once it got dark. State officials called for the National Guard to come in and watch the protesters. But people all over the world—from every race, gender, and age—had enough. They continued protesting. They weren't saying that other races didn't matter. They wanted police officers, teachers, doctors, judges, and even the president of the United States of America to remember that Black lives mattered, too.

CHAPTER 5
Black Futures Matter

The protests after George Floyd's murder weren't just about police brutality. What happened to George Floyd on that terrible day started a larger conversation. There is a long history of Black people being mistreated in the United States, ever since West Africans were brought here against their will. They were sold and forced into free labor, called slavery, to help build the United States. Black people were never paid for their hard work. But the work they did helped many white people prosper.

Shortly after slavery ended, many ideas were put into action that kept Black people from improving their lives. These ideas created what is known as systemic—or institutional—

racism. Government agencies in the United States used a red marker to outline sections of cities where mostly Black people lived, and then specifically denied services to residents in those areas, which often meant cheaper housing, worse roads, and fewer shops. This is called redlining.

Redlined segregation limited educational opportunities, which forced Black people into lower-paying jobs.

White people were more likely to be elected to political positions, which allowed them to create and change laws that benefitted them. This, in turn, created many other kinds of institutional racism.

For example: Black people are more often racially profiled by police officers than other citizens. Black people have also been given harsher prison sentences for the same crimes that white people commit. This means that prisons are filled with more Black people than any other race.

The Black Lives Matter movement has come up with many ways to push back against systemic racism. The main way is by investing in Black futures. Every February during Black History Month, Black Futures Month challenges the community to imagine a world in which Black people are free to simply experience joy. What does that look like? Black Lives Matter Arts+Culture provides opportunities for the world to experience Black joy through art, performances, and music.

For Alicia, Patrisse, Opal, and every person involved in the Black Lives Matter movement, changing the way Black people see the world and themselves is one big way to free themselves from white supremacy and oppression.

On April 20, 2021, a jury found Derek

Chauvin guilty of murdering George Floyd. Although justice had finally been served for George Floyd, there is still more work to do. The Black Lives Matter movement will continue to work on changing the way Black people are treated by the police and the world.

Timeline of the Black Lives Matter Movement

2012 — George Zimmerman shoots Trayvon Martin in Sanford, Florida

2013 — George Zimmerman is acquitted of the murder of Trayvon Martin

— Alicia Garza and Patrisse Cullors create the #BlackLivesMatter hashtag in a Facebook post that urged people to stop giving up on Black life

2014 — The murder of Michael Brown sparks massive protests in Ferguson, Missouri, and across the country

— Black Life Matters Riders take buses to Ferguson, Missouri, in support of protesters

2015 — *Essence* magazine dedicates their cover to Black Lives Matter

2016 — NFL players kneel during the national anthem to support #BlackLivesMatter

2020 — During the global COVID-19 pandemic, George Floyd dies when a police officer kneels on his neck for nine minutes and twenty-nine seconds

— A worldwide protest goes on for weeks as people leave their homes in the middle of a pandemic to protest the unjust death of George Floyd

2021 — Officer Derek Chauvin is tried and found guilty of murdering George Floyd

Timeline of the World

2012 — Barack Obama is reelected for a second term as the president of the United States of America

— Summer Olympics take place in London, England

2013 — The word *selfie* is added to the dictionary

— Former South African president and leader of the anti-apartheid movement Nelson Mandela dies

2014 — The robot lander module Philae completes the first-ever comet landing

2015 — The world comes together to strike a deal on climate change

2018 — Ángela Maria Ponce Camacho is the first transgender woman to win the title of Miss Spain and is also the first to compete for the Miss Universe title

2020 — The novel coronavirus disease COVID-19 spreads all over the world, sickening and killing millions of people

2021 — Kamala Harris is sworn in as the first female vice president of the United States of America

Bibliography

*Books for young readers

Khan-Cullors, Patrisse, and Asha Bandele. *When They Call You a Terrorist: A Story of Black Lives Matter and the Power to Change the World*. New York: St. Martin's Press, 2020.

Lawson, Steven F. *Running for Freedom: Civil Rights and Black Politics in America since 1941*. Malden, MA: Wiley, 2014.

McIvor, David Wallace. *Mourning in America: Race and the Politics of Loss*. Ithaca, NY: Cornell University Press, 2016.

*Reynolds, Jason, and Ibram X. Kendi. *Stamped: Racism, Antiracism, and You: A Remix of the National Book Award–Winning Stamped from the Beginning*. New York: Little, Brown and Company, 2020.

*Reynolds, Jason, Ibram X. Kendi, and Sonja Cherry-Paul. *Stamped (for Kids): Racism, Antiracism, and You*. Illustrated by Rachelle Baker. New York: Little, Brown and Company, 2021.

*Rhodes, Jewell Parker. *Ghost Boys*. New York: Little, Brown and Company, 2018.

*Tyner, Artika R. *Black Lives Matter: From Hashtag to the Streets*. The Fight for Black Rights. Minneapolis, MN: Lerner Publications, 2021.

*Tyner, Artika R. *Vigilante Danger: A Threat to Black Lives*. The Fight for Black Rights. Minneapolis, MN: Lerner Publications, 2021.

Yancy, George, and Janine Jones, eds. *Pursuing Trayvon Martin: Historical Contexts and Contemporary Manifestations*. Lanham, MD: Lexington Books, 2012.